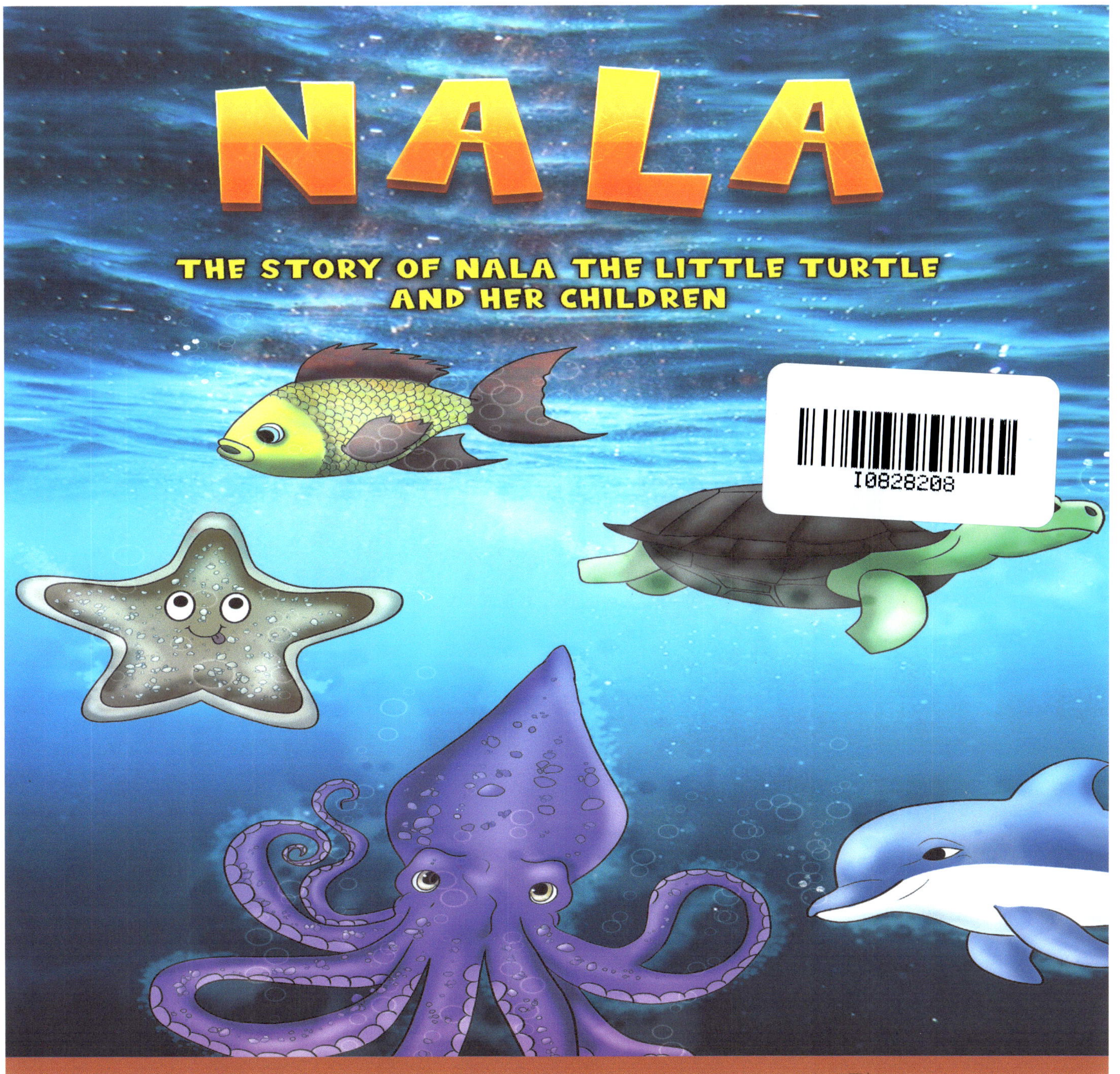
NALA
THE STORY OF NALA THE LITTLE TURTLE
AND HER CHILDREN
WRITTEN BY DELIA IABONI

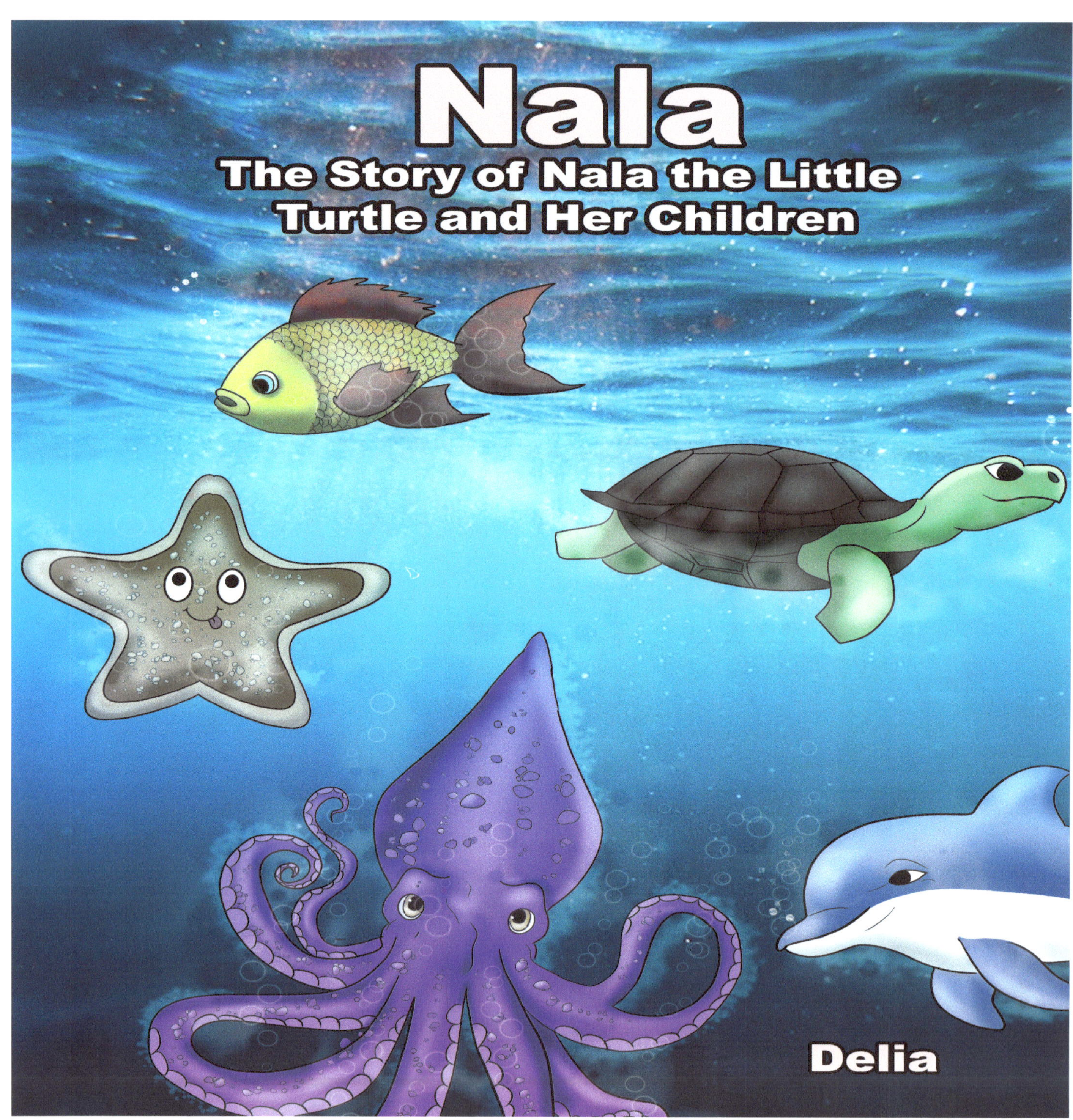
Nala
The Story of Nala the Little
Turtle and Her Children
Delia

This book is dedicated to all the people who make this world better.

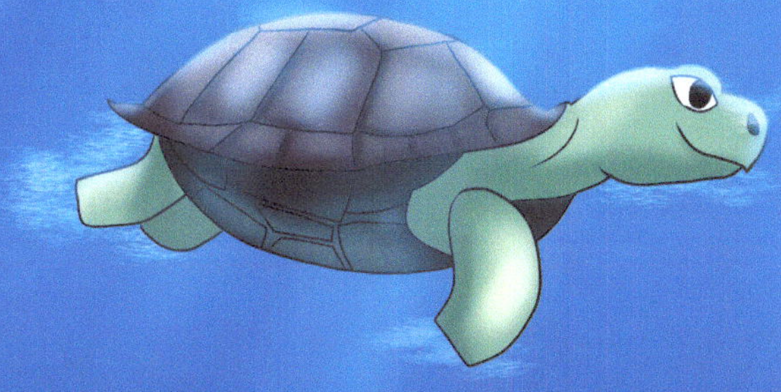

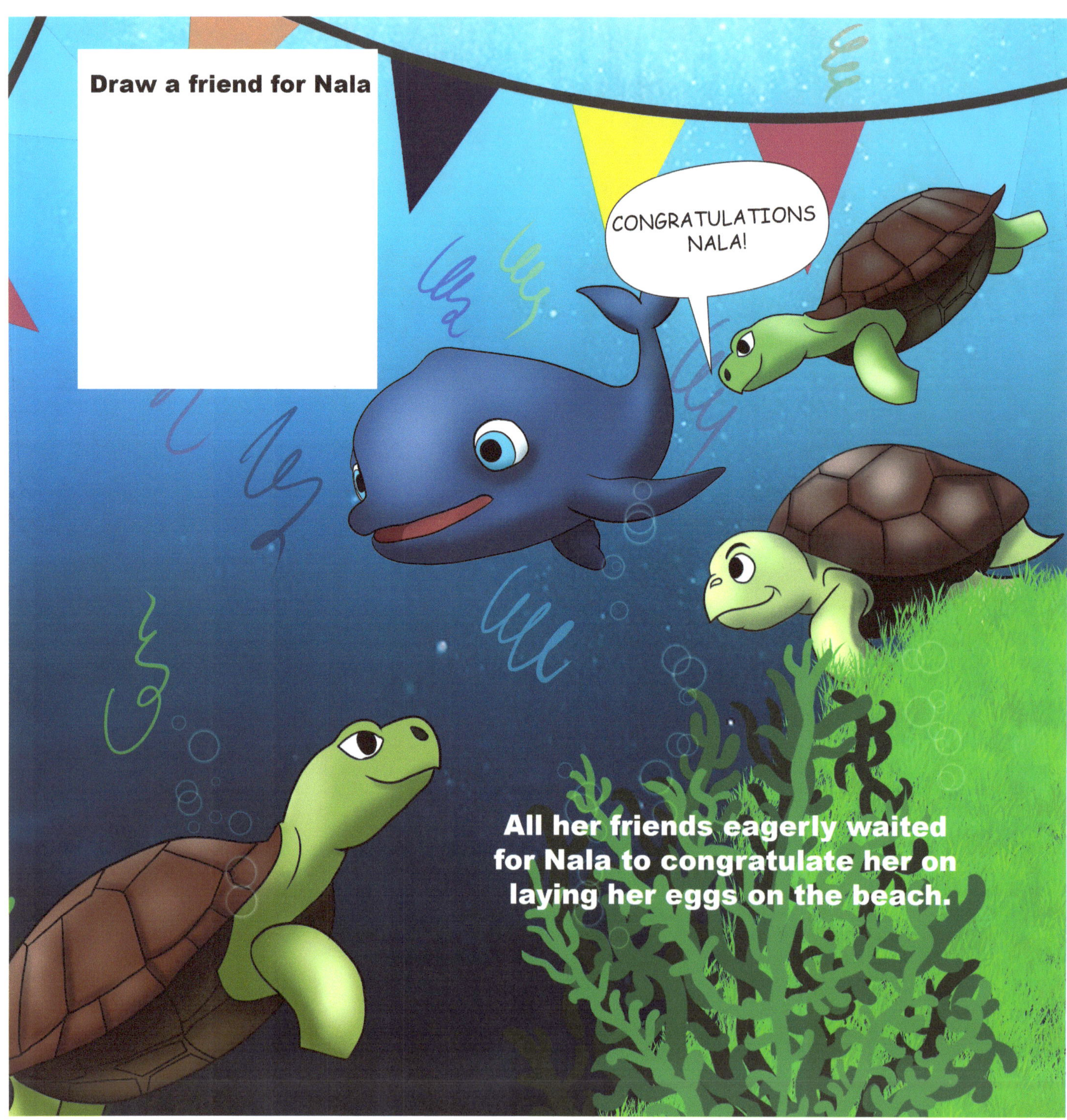
Draw a friend for Nala
CONGRATULATIONS
NALA!
All her friends eagerly waited
for Nala to congratulate her on
laying her eggs on the beach.

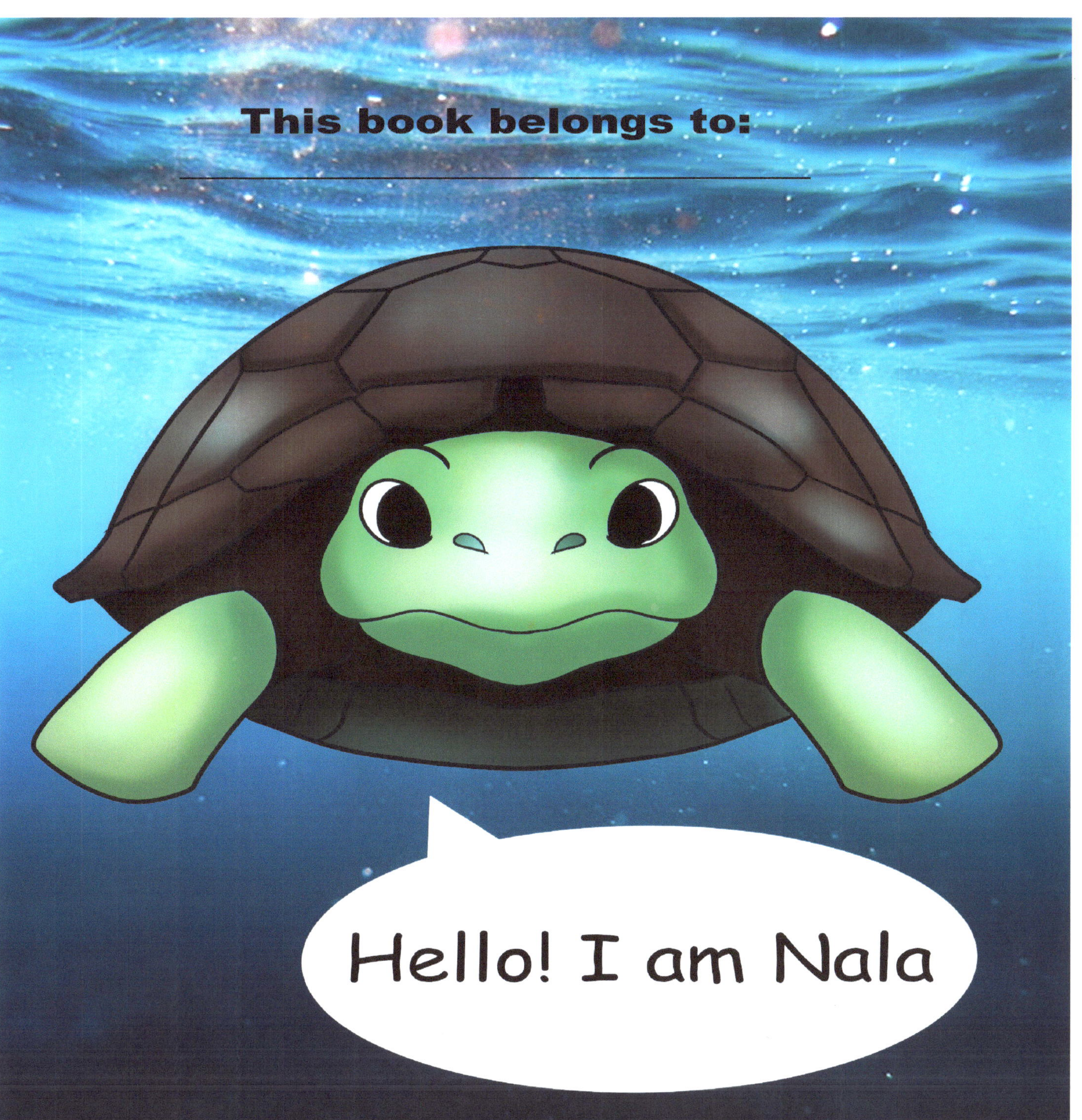
This book belongs to:
Hello! I am Nala

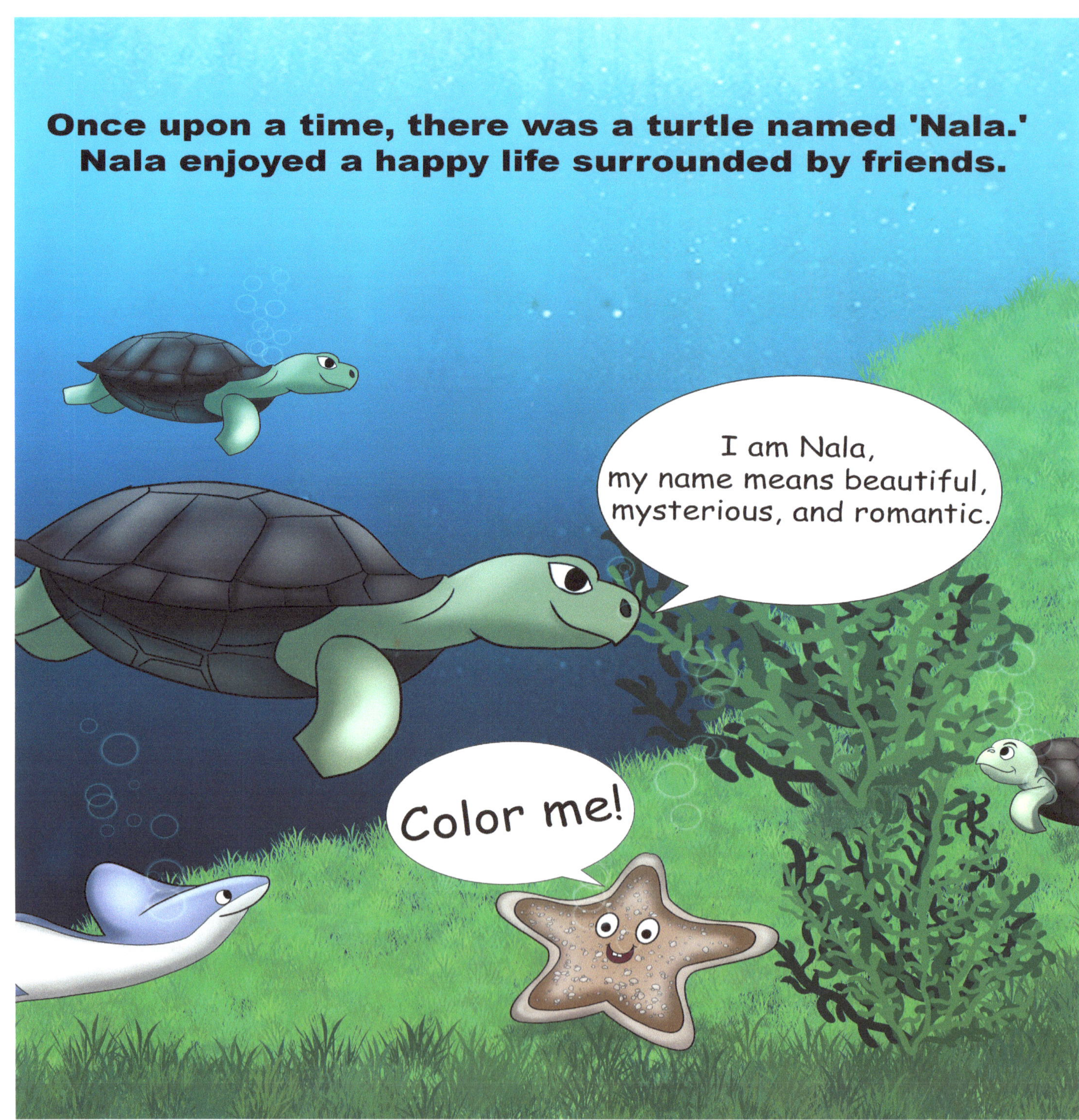
Once upon a time, there was a turtle named 'Nala.'
Nala enjoyed a happy life surrounded by friends.
I am Nala,
my name means beautiful,
mysterious, and romantic.
Color me!

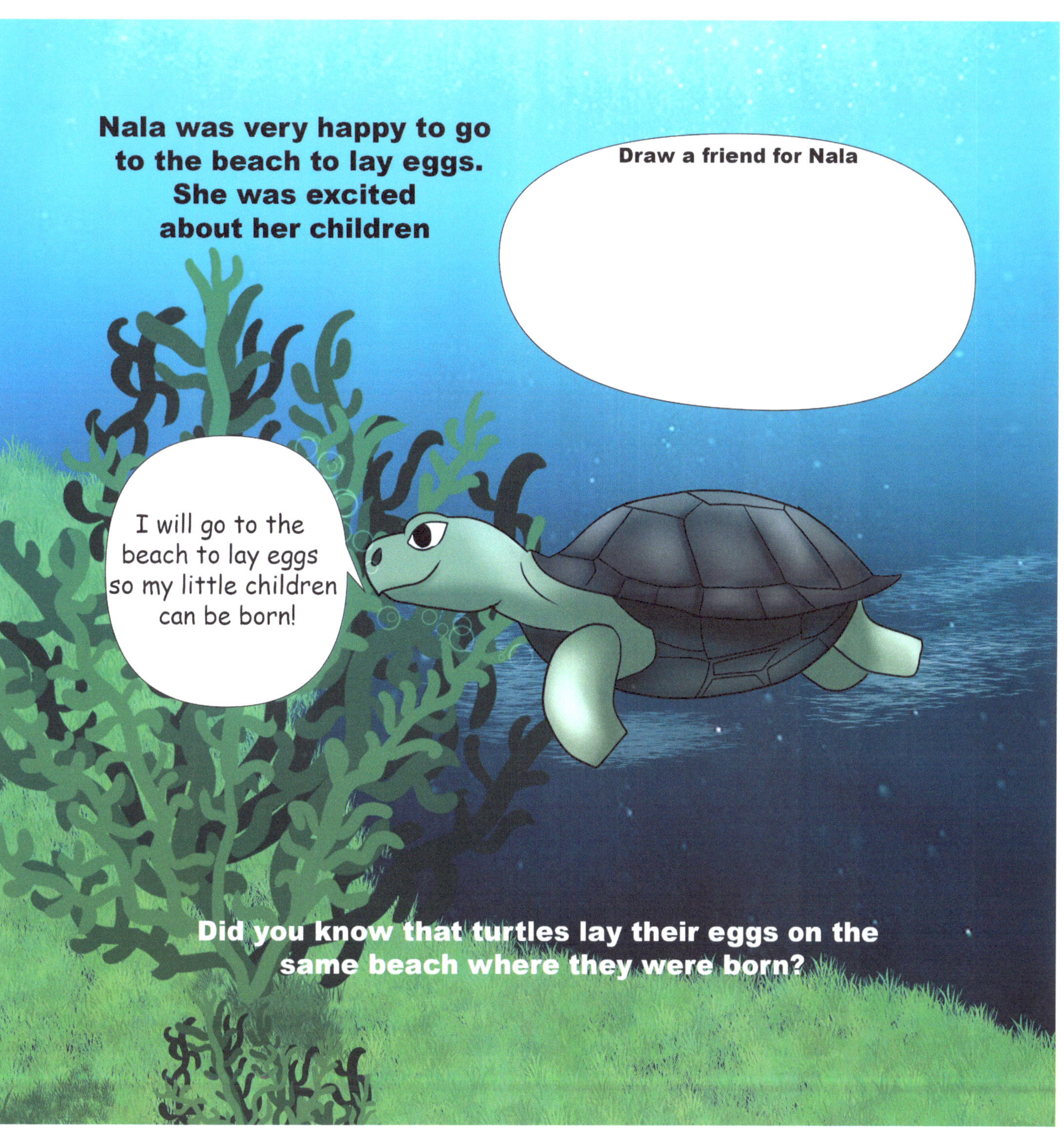
Nala was very happy to go to the beach to lay eggs. She was excited about her children
Draw a friend for Nala
I will go to the beach to lay eggs so my little children can be born!
Did you know that turtles lay their eggs on the same beach where they were born?

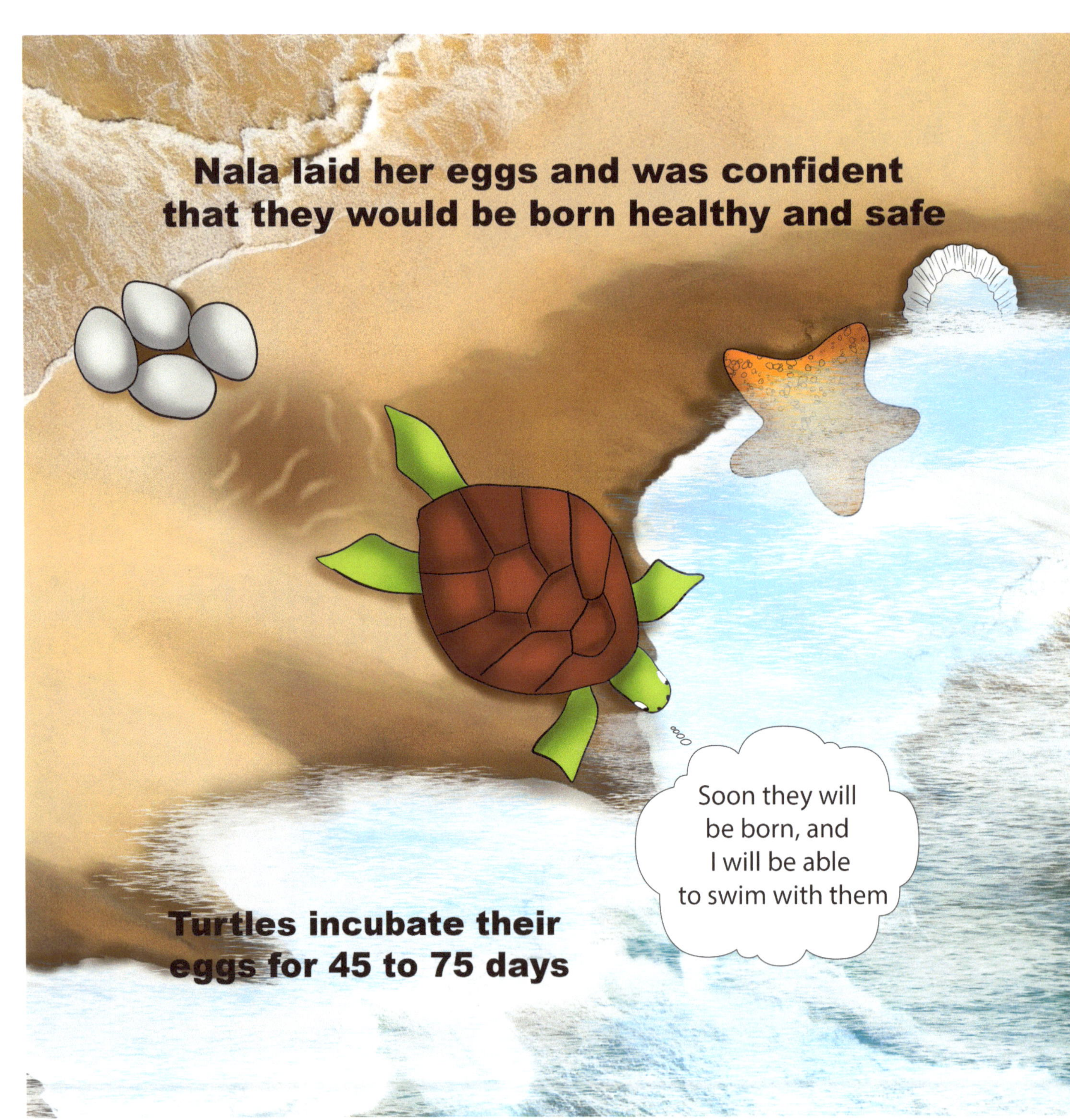
Nala laid her eggs and was confident that they would be born healthy and safe
Soon they will be born, and I will be able to swim with them
Turtles incubate their eggs for 45 to 75 days

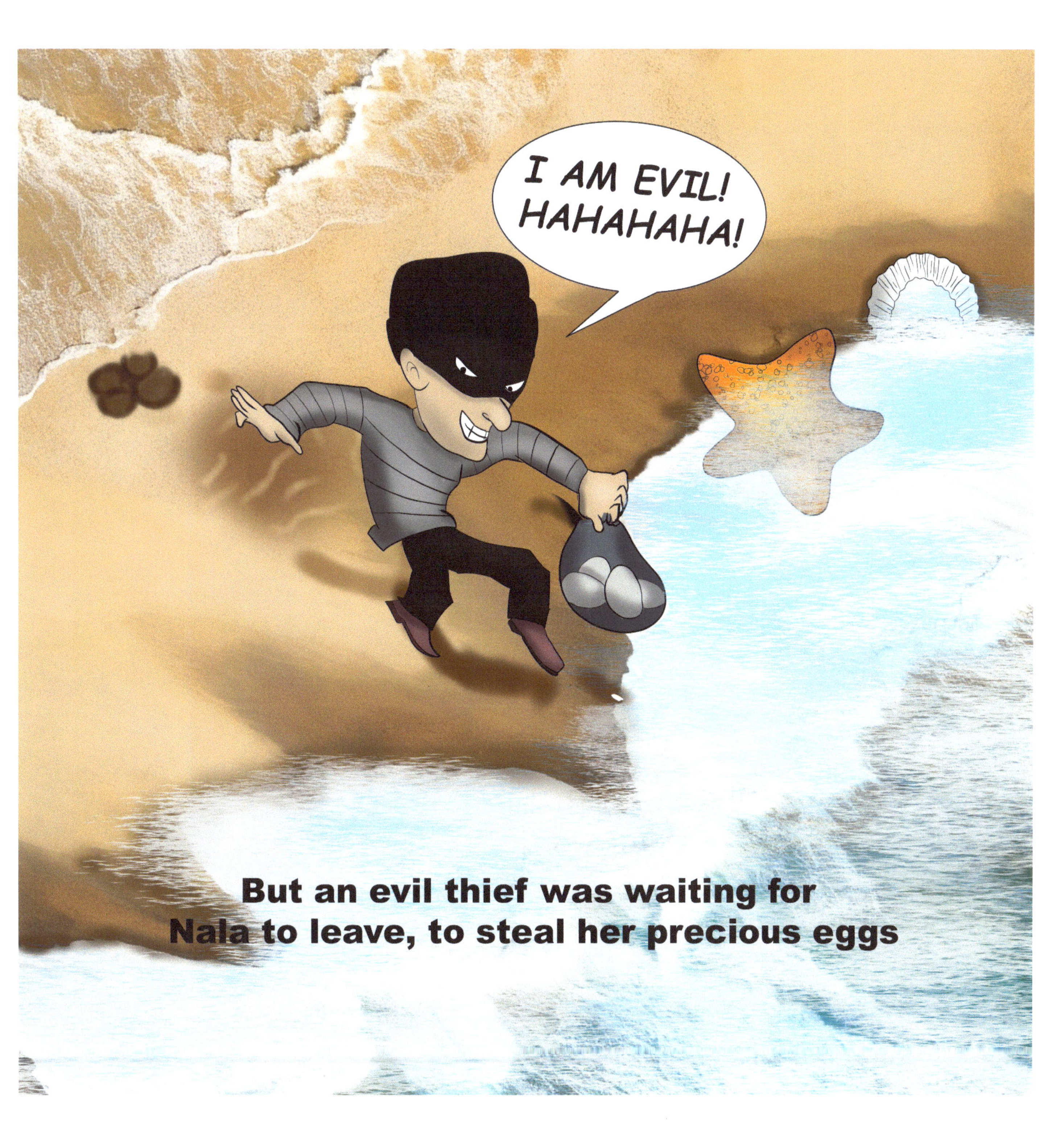
I AM EVIL!
HAHAHAHA!
But an evil thief was waiting for
Nala to leave, to steal her precious eggs

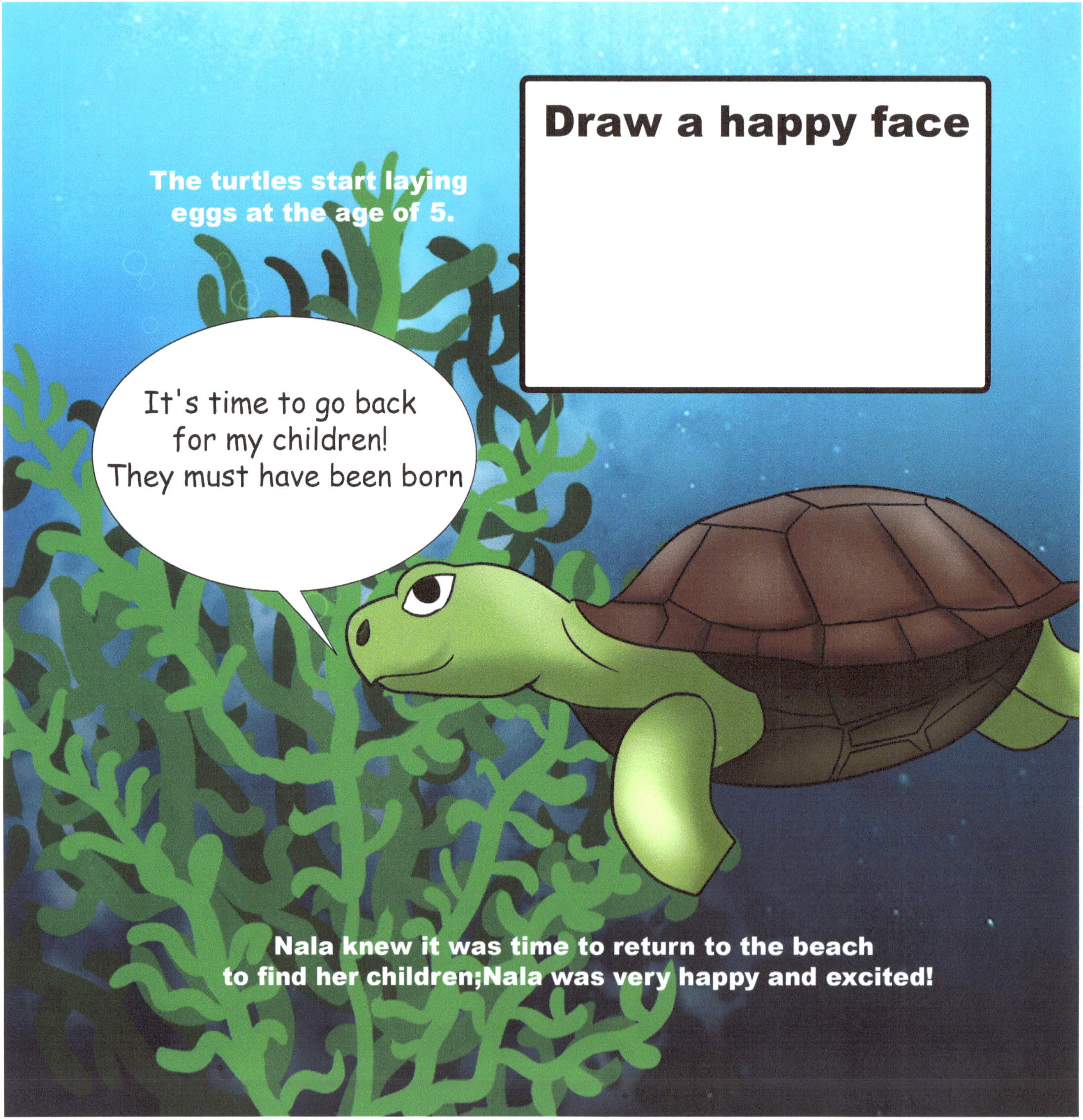

The turtles start laying eggs at the age of 5.

Draw a happy face

It's time to go back for my children! They must have been born

Nala knew it was time to return to the beach to find her children;Nala was very happy and excited!

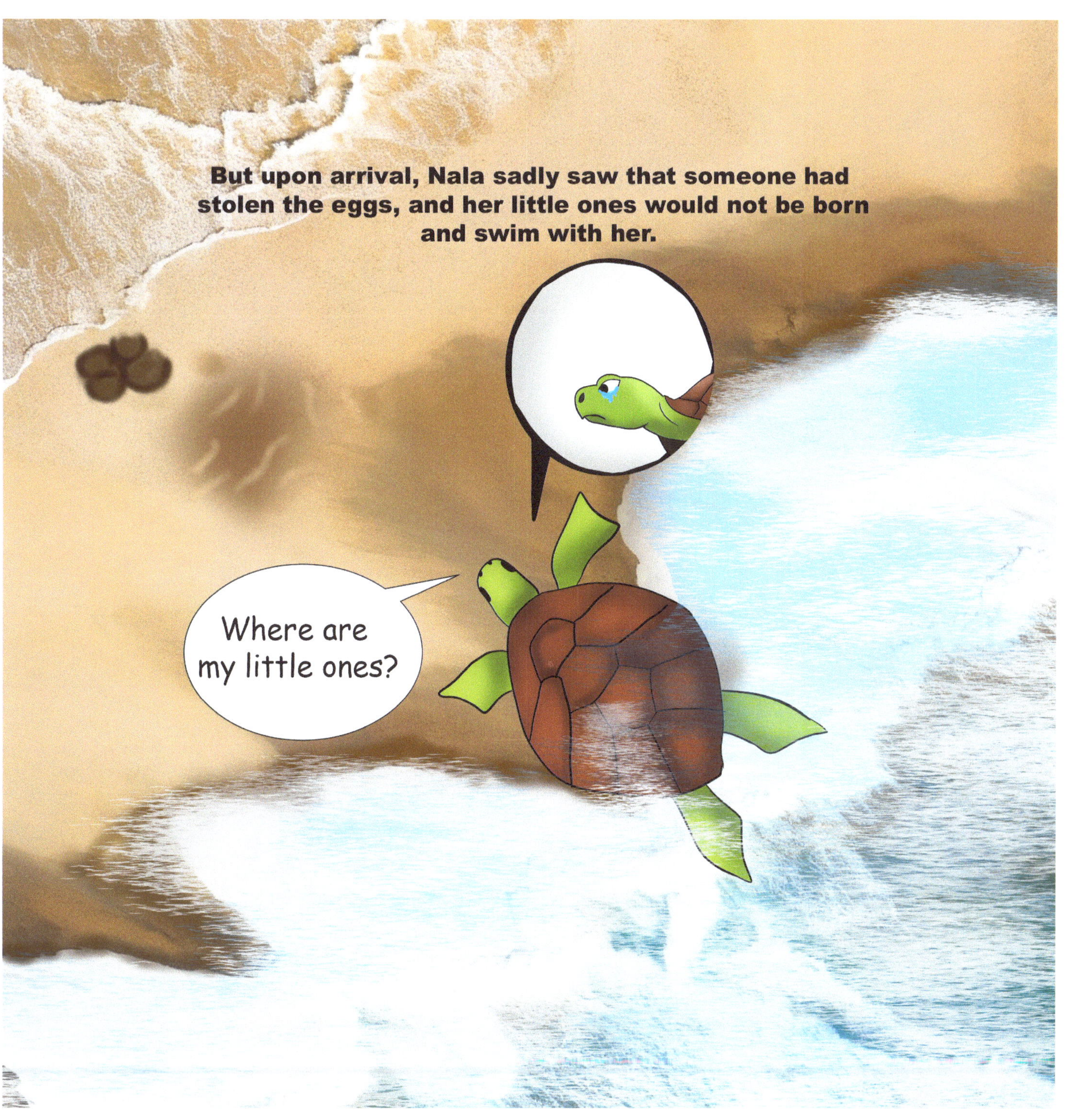
But upon arrival, Nala sadly saw that someone had stolen the eggs, and her little ones would not be born and swim with her.
Where are my little ones?

Nala swam to the bottom of the sea to be alone. She was so sad to have lost her little ones that she didn't want to be with anyone.

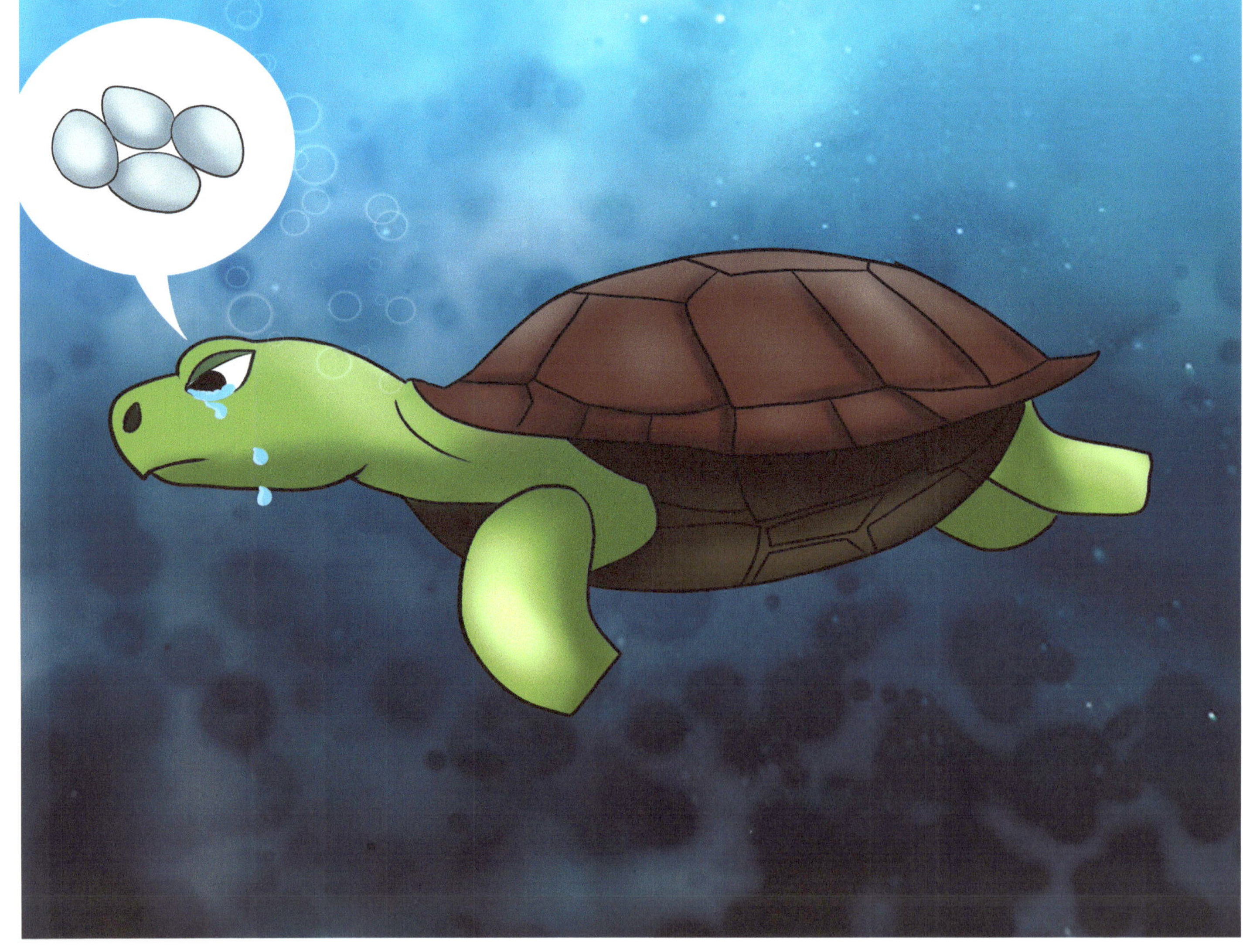

Nala's friends swam to console her.

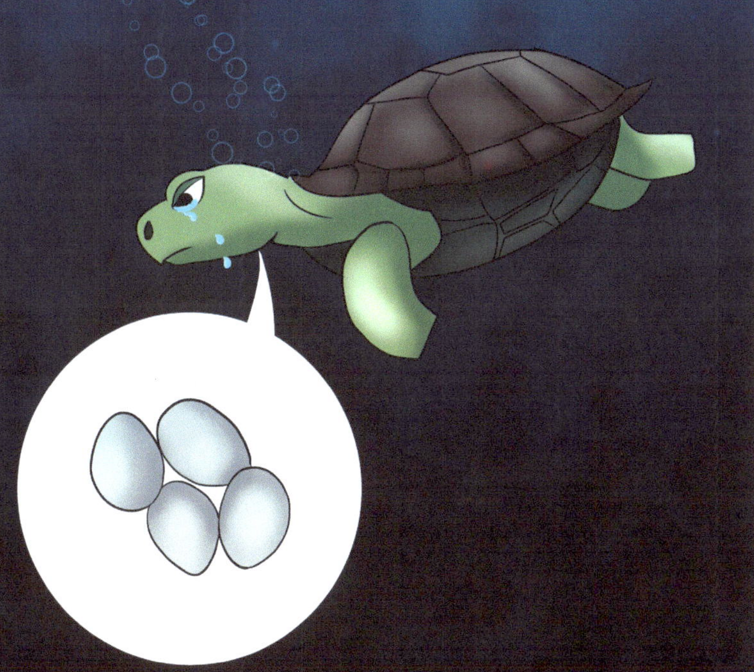

Draw her friends

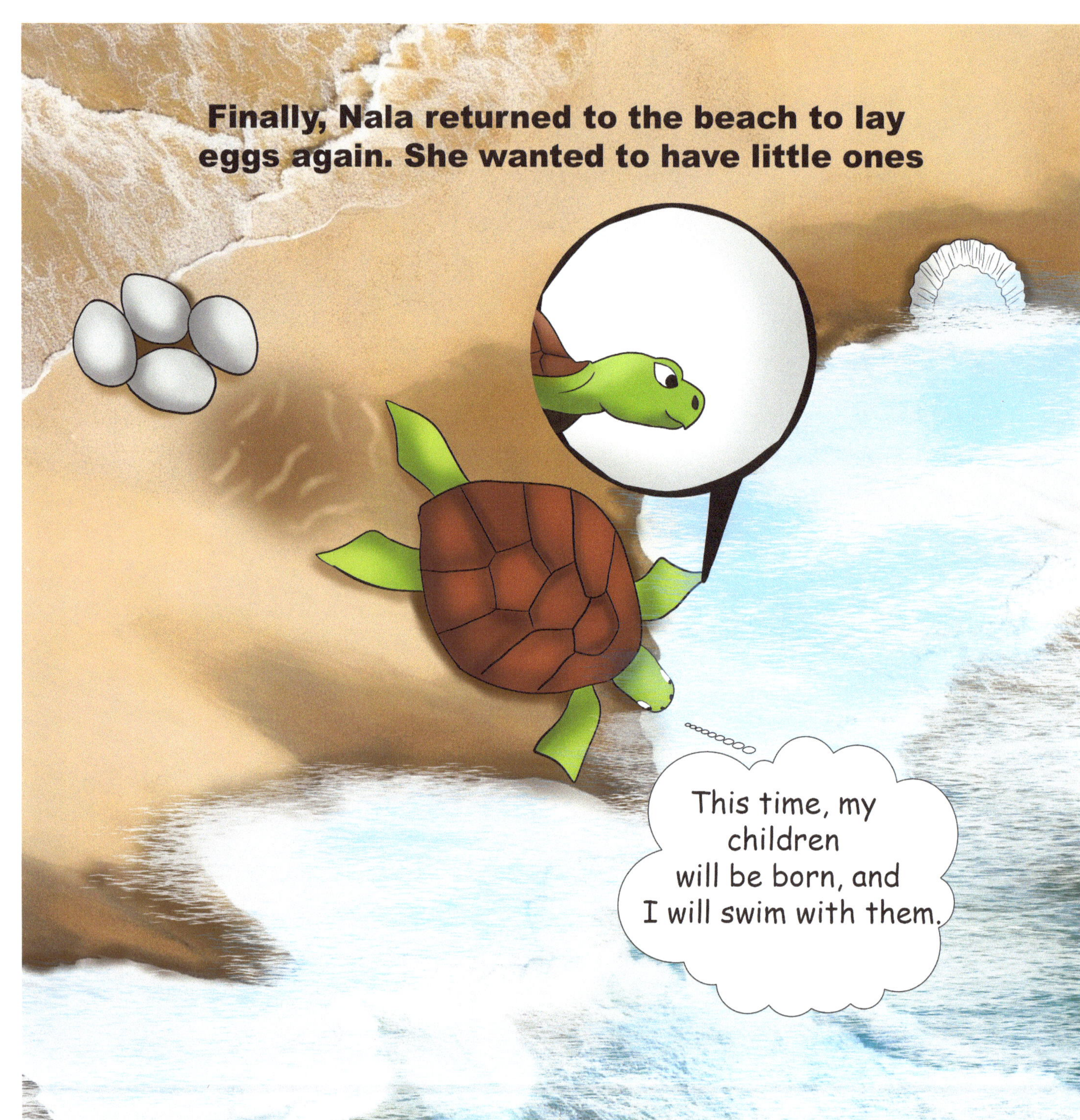
Finally, Nala returned to the beach to lay eggs again. She wanted to have little ones
This time, my children will be born, and I will swim with them.

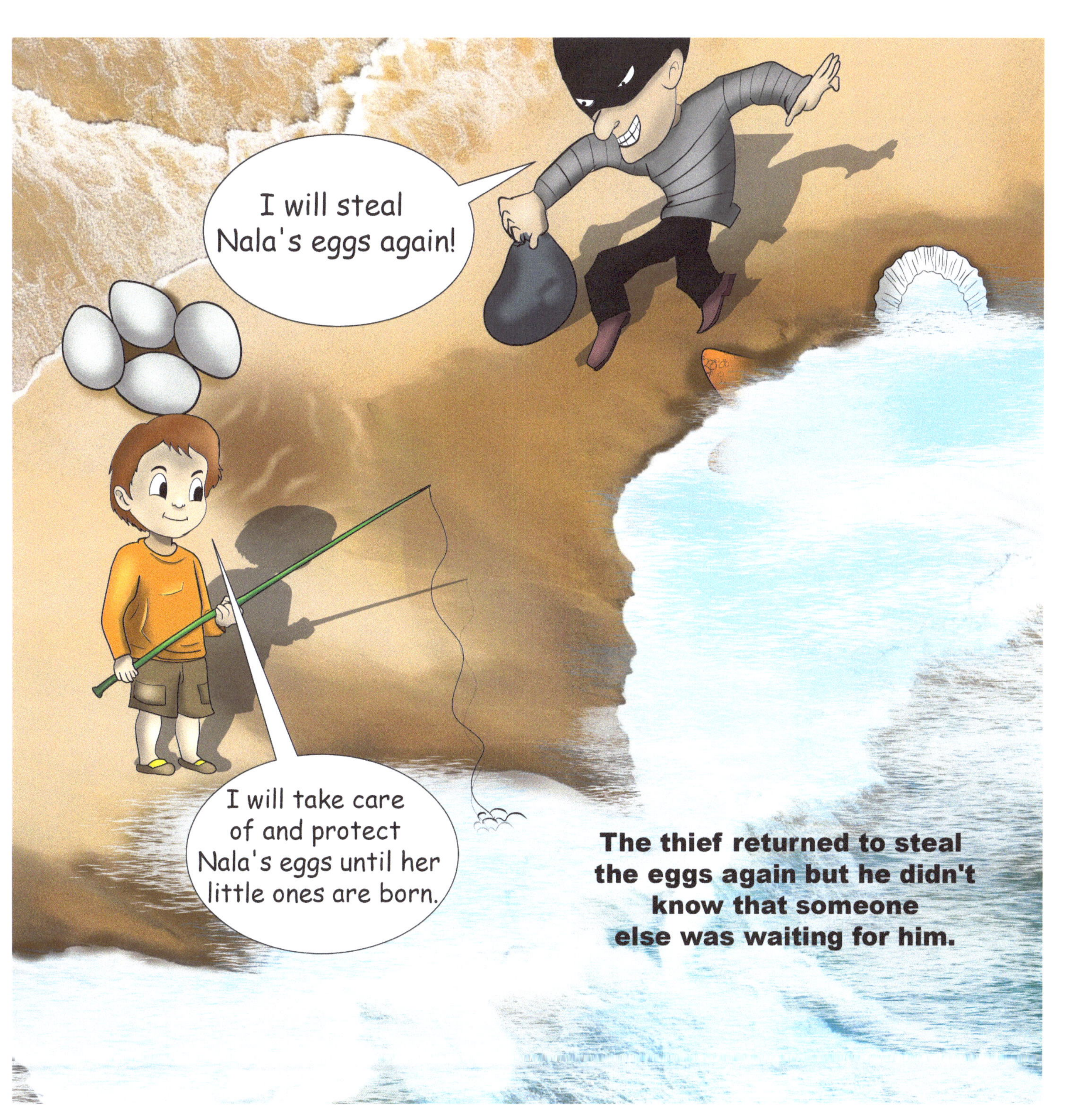
I will steal
Nala's eggs again!
I will take care
of and protect
Nala's eggs until her
little ones are born.
The thief returned to steal
the eggs again but he didn't
know that someone
else was waiting for him.

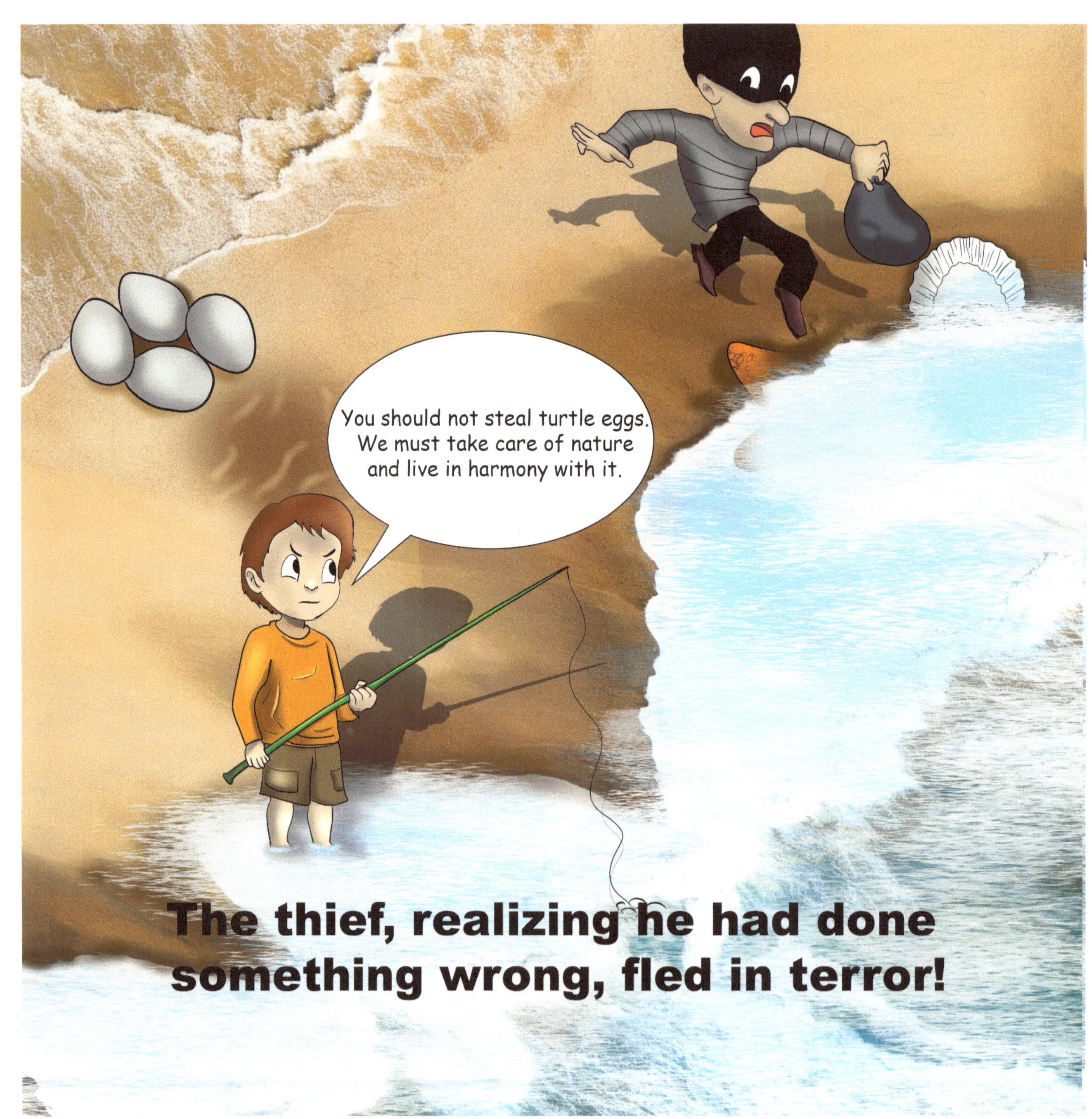

The thief, realizing he had done something wrong, fled in terror!

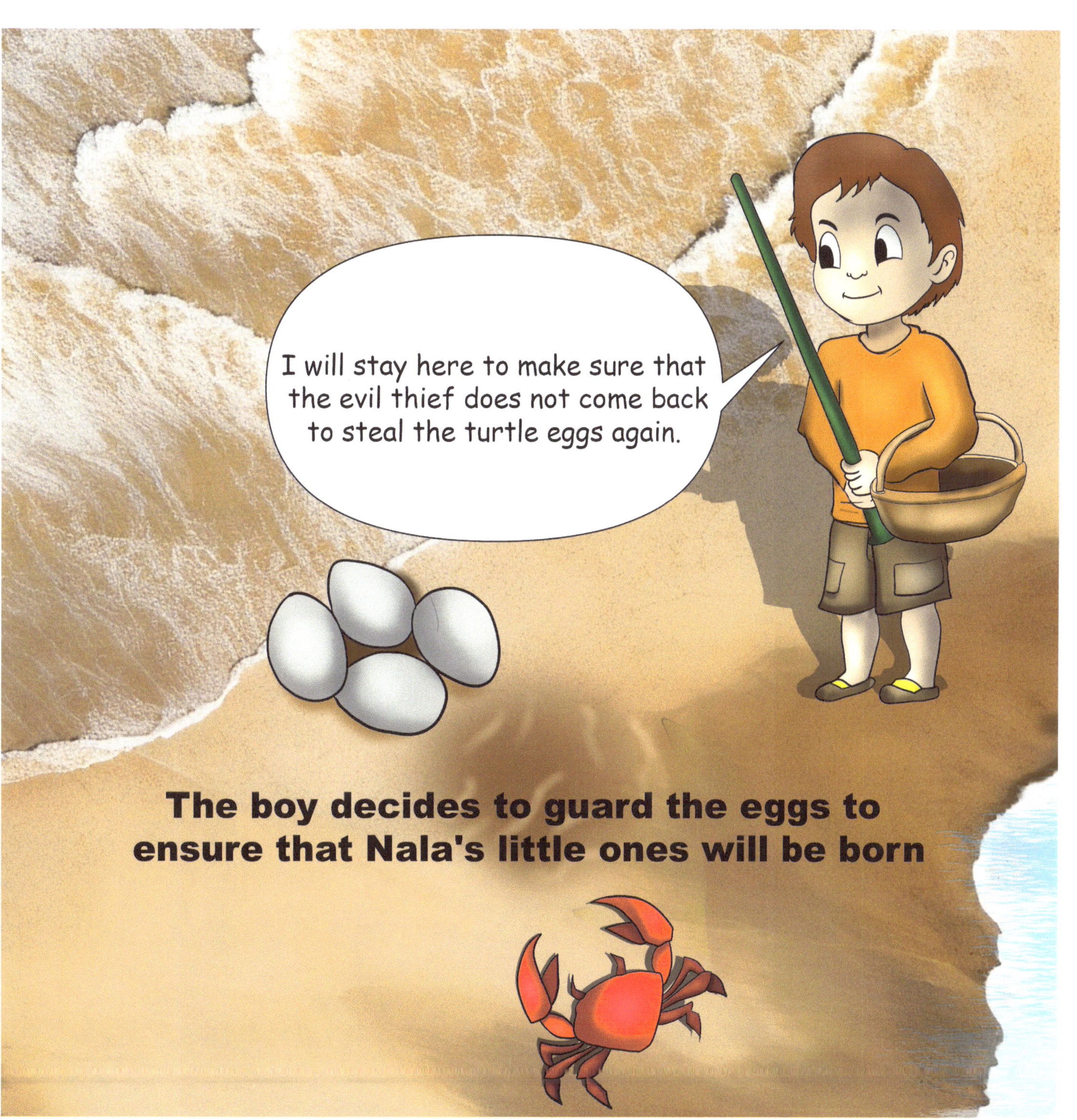
I will stay here to make sure that the evil thief does not come back to steal the turtle eggs again.
The boy decides to guard the eggs to ensure that Nala's little ones will be born

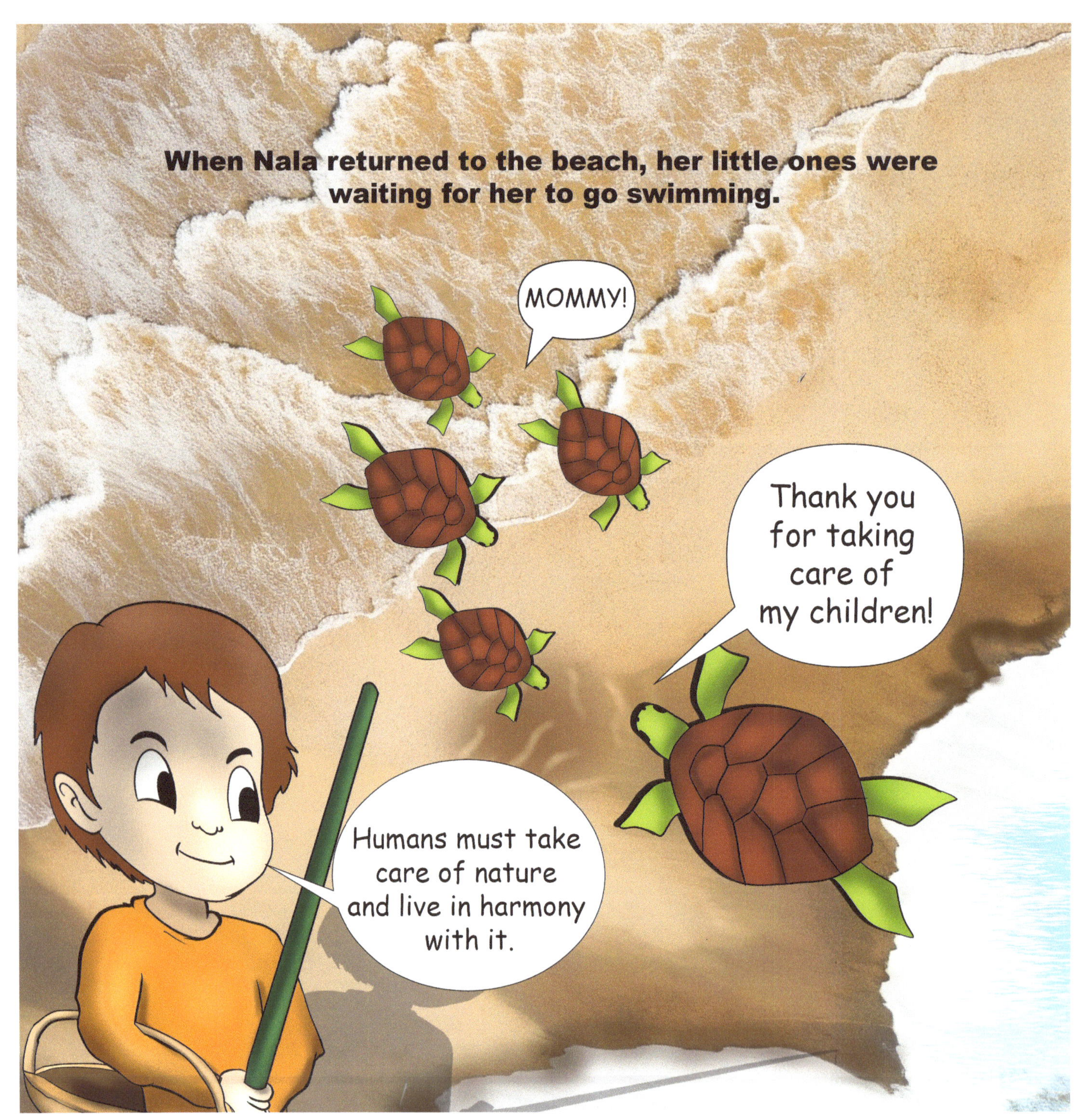
When Nala returned to the beach, her little ones were waiting for her to go swimming.
MOMMY!
Thank you for taking care of my children!
Humans must take care of nature and live in harmony with it.

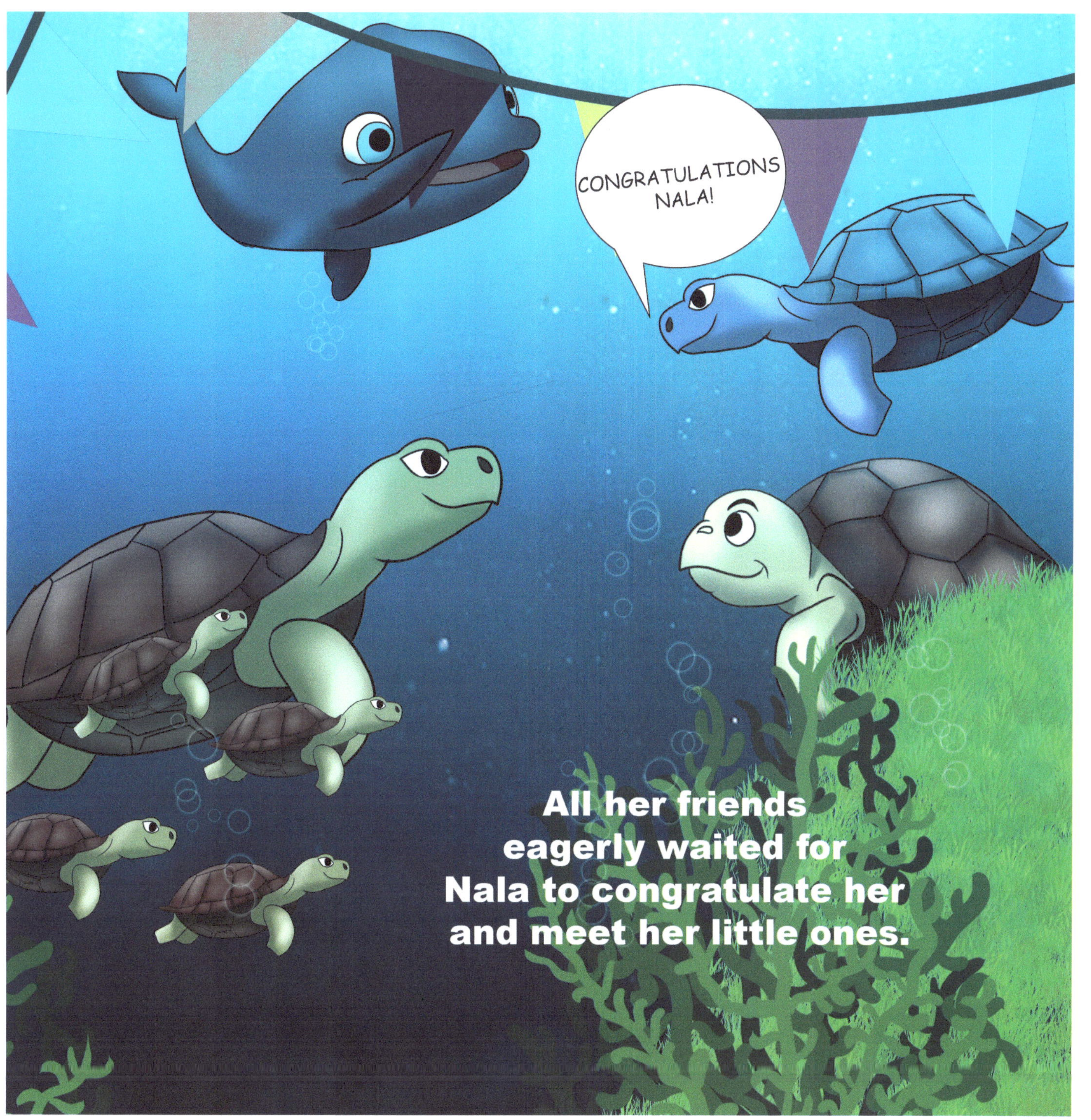

All her friends
eagerly waited for
Nala to congratulate her
and meet her little ones.

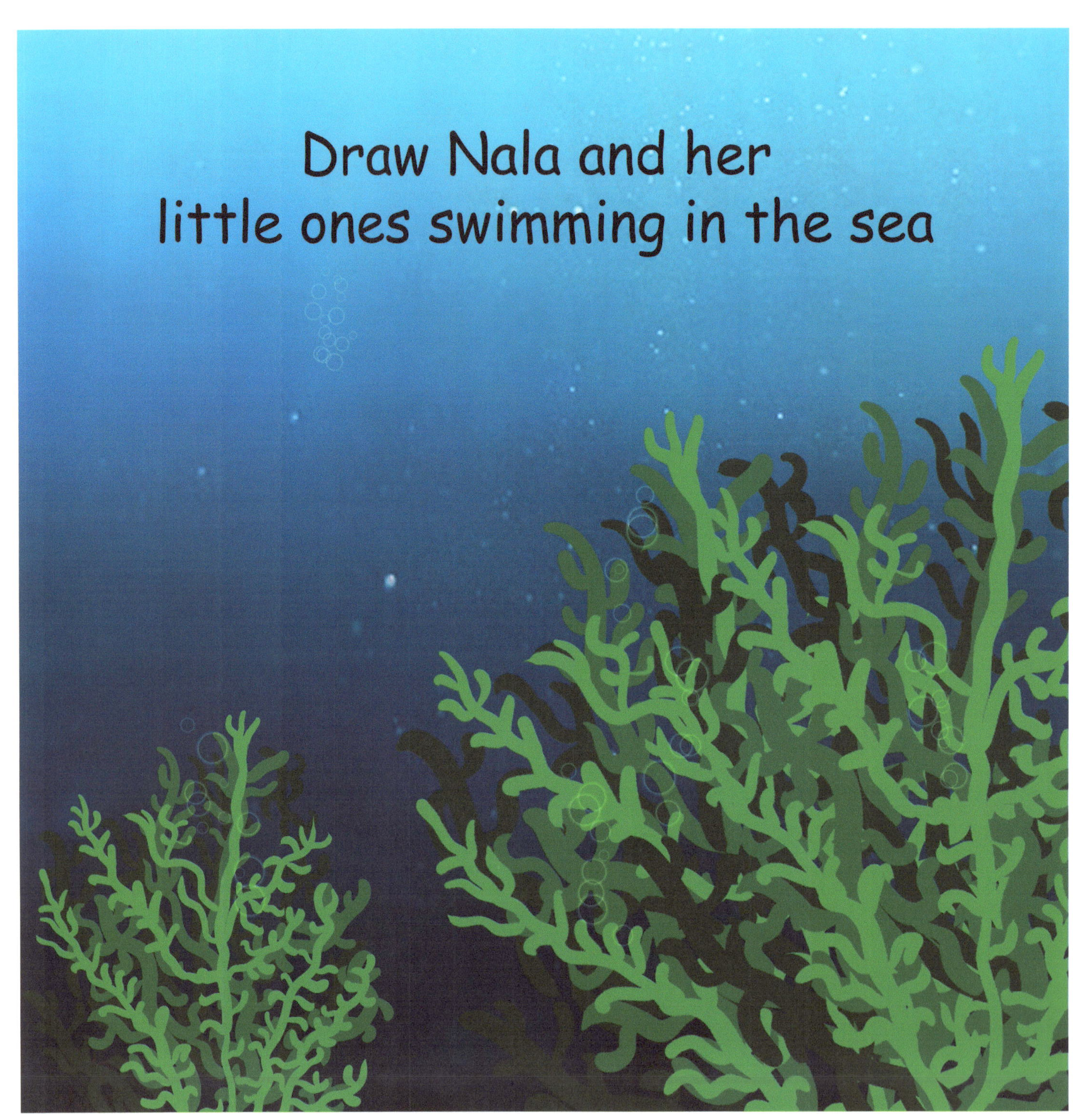
Draw Nala and her
little ones swimming in the sea

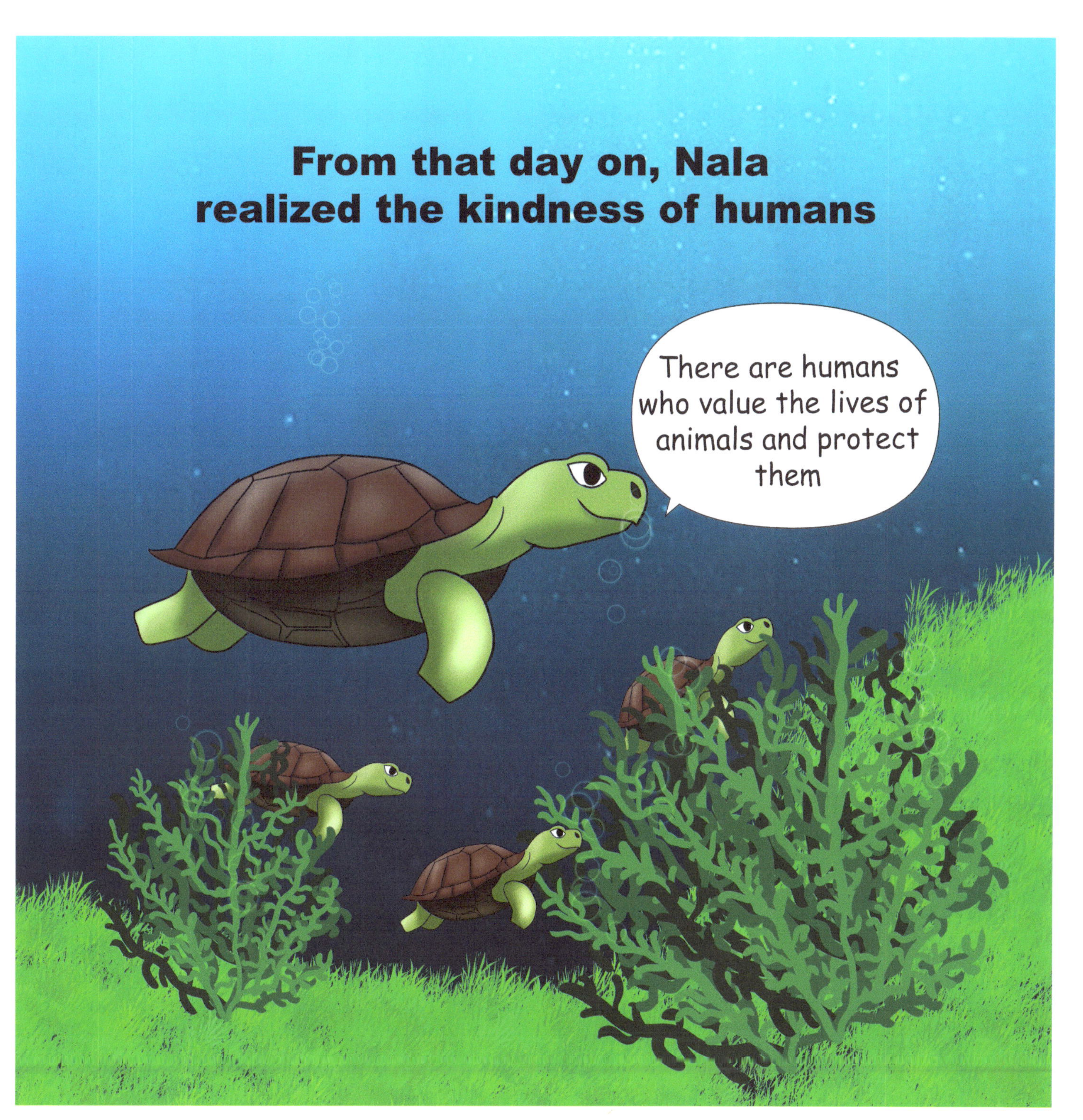
From that day on, Nala
realized the kindness of humans
There are humans who value the lives of animals and protect them

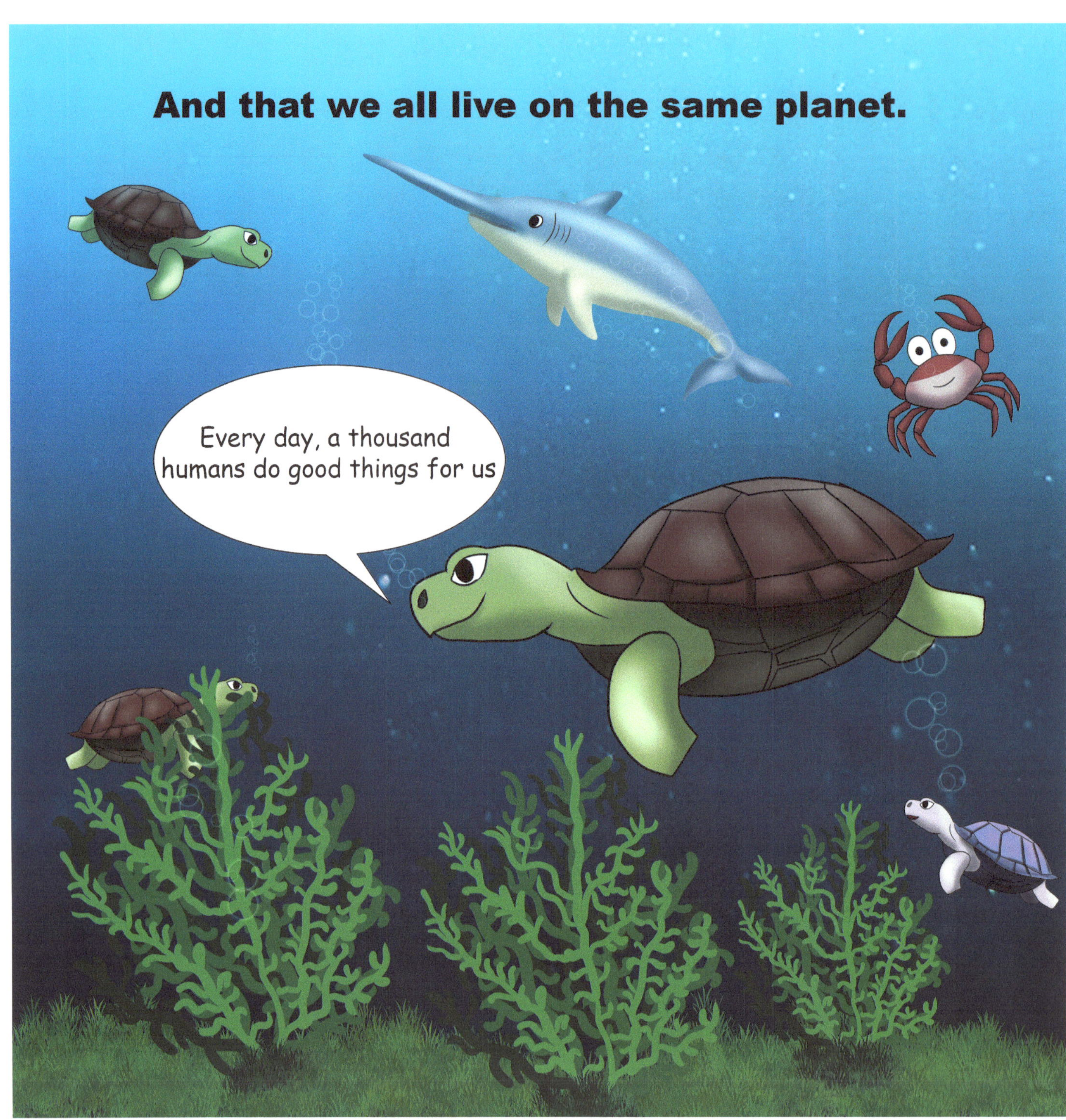
And that we all live on the same planet.
Every day, a thousand humans do good things for us

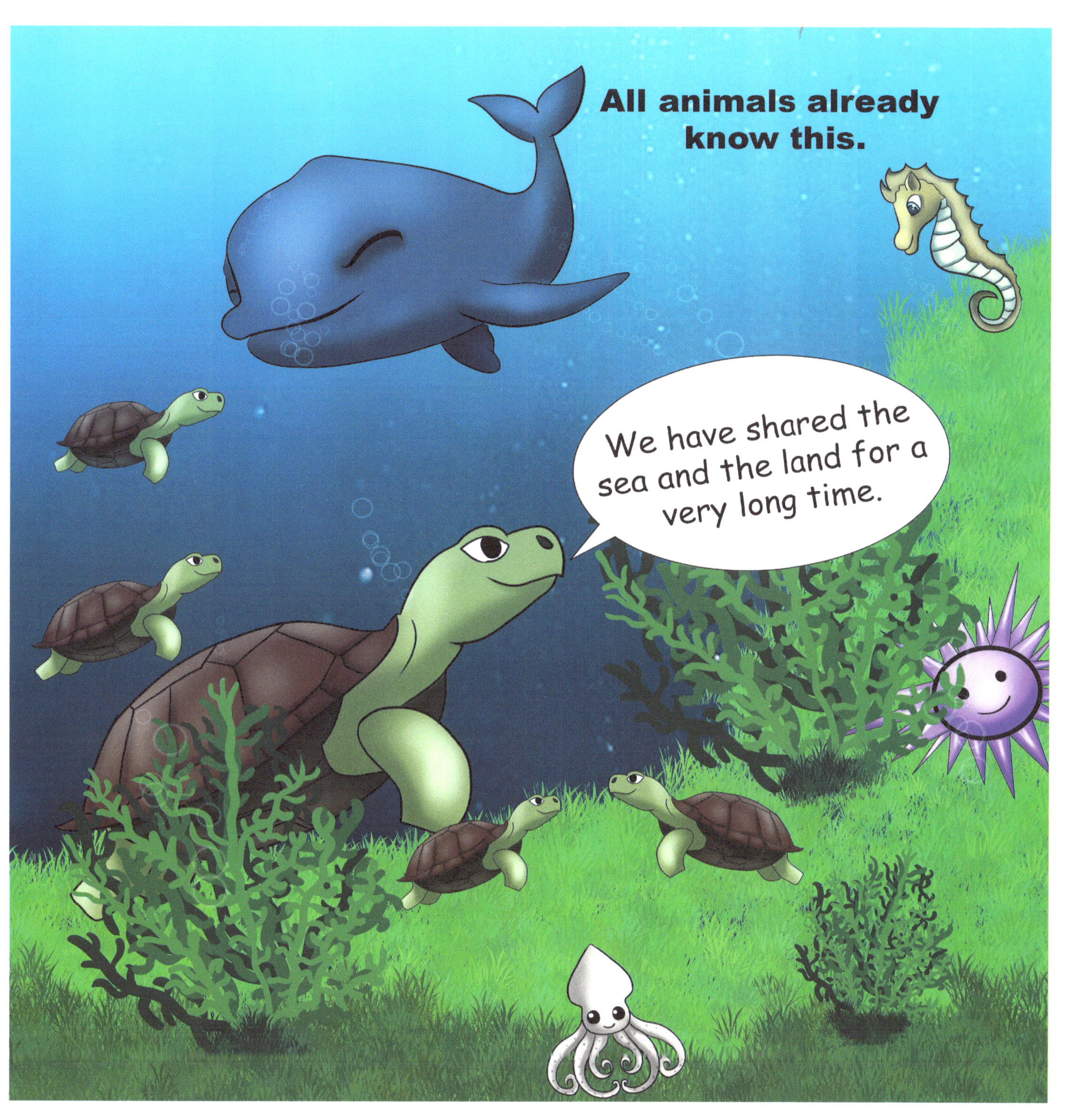
All animals already know this.
We have shared the sea and the land for a very long time.

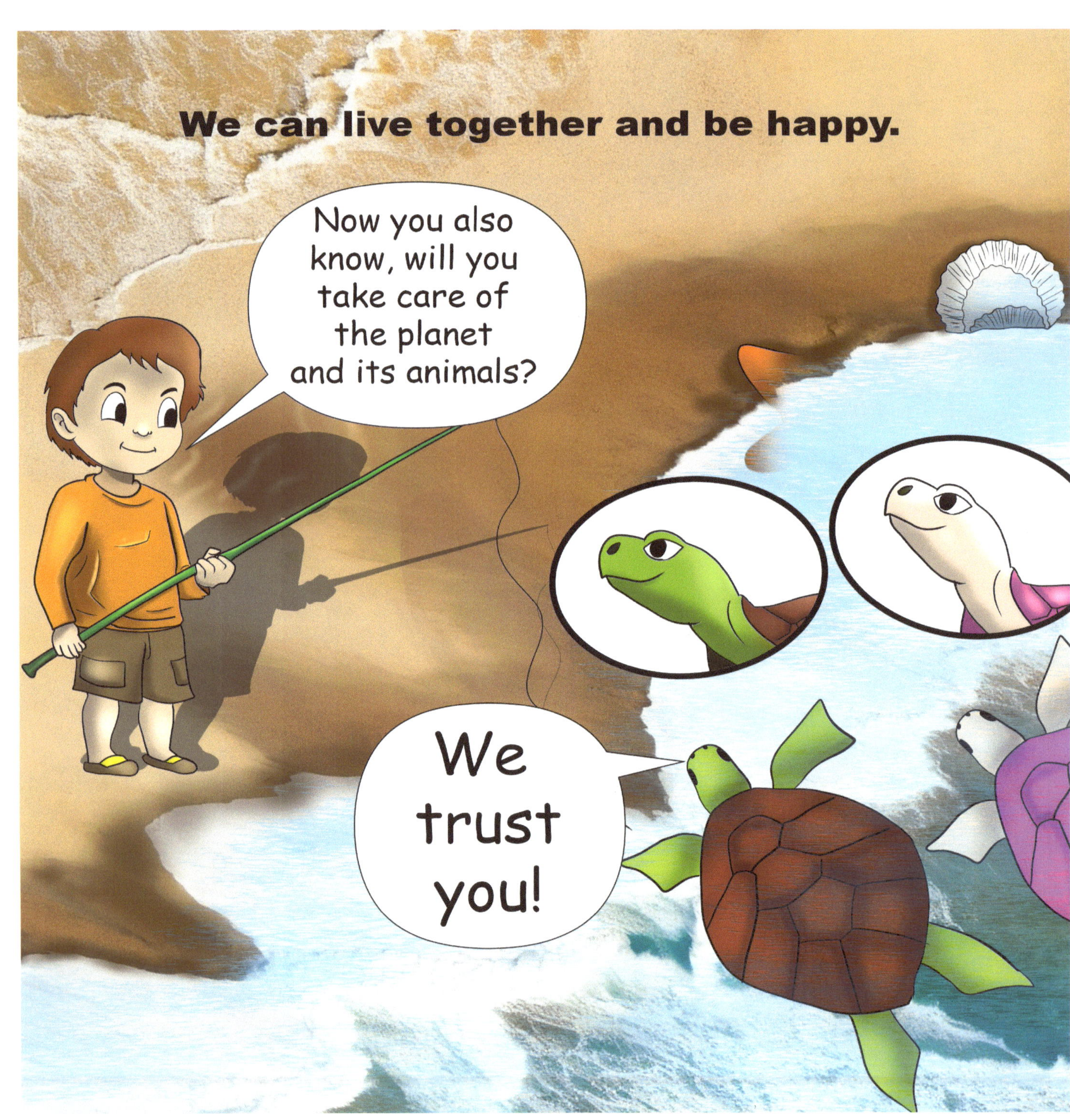
We can live together and be happy.
Now you also know, will you take care of the planet and its animals?
We trust you!

www.ingramcontent.com/pod-product-compliance
Lightning Source LLC
LaVergne TN
LVHW070225110826
845147LV00003B/650
9781964630151